MW00451248

Rocket Launches -- "All About This & That" Picture Book
by Adrian D. Robbe

All Rights Reserved. Copyright © 2018 by Adrian D. Robbe
Published by Adrian D. Robbe

Book Description: *Rocket Launches* is Volume 4 of the "All About This & That" Picture Book Series for Children by Adrian D. Robbe. This book has a wide assortment of specially selected photographs of actual rocket launches that occurred over the past 10 decades. The pictures with the accompanying facts form a rocket history timeline that depicts the significant advances that were made in rocket science. Designed primarily for children ages 7 to 12 years old, each picture in this book is accompanied by interesting and amazing facts about the history of rocket launches in support of space exploration.

Facts Presented: The facts presented in this book contain basic, fundamental, elementary information about rocket launches that are widely known. The information is common knowledge that is generally known to an educated reader.

Learning Benefits for Children: *Rocket Launches* -- "All About This & That" Picture Book Series for Children -- Volume 4 provides young children with an unforgettable learning adventure into the amazing wonders of rocket history and space exploration. The brief facts presented on rocket launches in this book serve as a simple, fun-to-read, learning adventure for children. The increased awareness that young boys and girls receive about rocket launches in this fascinating picture book will help them gain a greater appreciation about the marvelous world we live in.

Image Credits: Photo images used in this publication were obtained from the "NASA on the Commons" Flickr Website as well as Pixabay. The pictures from NASA have no known copyright restrictions. Images from Pixabay are free of copyrights and are released under the Creative Commons License CC0 into the public domain.

Disclaimer: *Rocket Launches* -- "All About This & That" Picture Book Series for Children (Volume 4) is neither authorized nor endorsed (explicitly or implicitly) by the National Aeronautics and Space Administration (NASA).

Copyright: This collective work is also a compilation based on photographic images and information made available to the general public. No claim of copyright is being made to any aspect of the source public domain images or information. However, the complete compilation and collection of images with the accompanying information in this book as a whole is considered protectable under the provision of 'collective works copyright' even though individual source images and information are not. Copyright protection of this collective compilation of data extends only to the selection, coordination, and arrangement of the materials and data, not to the data itself or the preexisting works themselves that are in the public domain. This collective work has changed the public domain material by doing the following: Used research, creativity, and a unique selection process in the choices and organization of public domain material by identifying: (1) the best story, (2) greatest photos, (3) most appropriate information, and (4) specific order of presentation to construct a specially designed compilation of information that was subsequently integrated into a single book format. For further information, see United States Copyright Office Circular 14 "Copyright in Derivative Works and Compilations."

Printed in the United States of America

ISBN 978-1-719-98152-1

Distribution Platform of Record: Amazon Digital Services LLC, 410 Terry Ave N, Seattle, WA 98109

1

Rocket Launches

Key questions answered, special topics, and other fun activities included in this book.

What is a rocket?

Simple Definition:
A rocket is "a vehicle put into orbit" (Dictionary.com) [1]

Scientific Definition:
A rocket is a "vehicle, typically cylindrical, containing liquid or solid propellants which produce hot gases or ions that are ejected rearward through a nozzle and, in doing so, create an action force accompanied by an opposite and equal reaction force driving the vehicle forward." [2]

Photo Credit: NASA

What are rockets used for?

Rockets can be used to carry <u>spacecraft</u> (such as research or communication <u>satellites</u>), space laboratories, as well as space stations for transporting human beings into space. Some spacecraft are designed with special scientific research equipment and can take close-up pictures of planets and other parts of the universe. Some spacecraft can go extremely far distances into outer space where humans are unable to travel.

Photo Credit: NASA

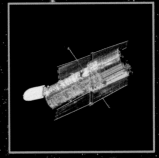

Photo Credit: NASA

1. <u>Satellite</u> - "A device designed to be launched into orbit around the earth, another planet, the sun, etc." (Dictionary.com) [3]
2. <u>Spacecraft</u> - "A spacecraft is a vehicle designed for travel or operation in space beyond the earth's atmosphere or in orbit around the earth." (Dictionary.com) [4]

How does a rocket engine work?

A rocket engine "produces <u>thrust</u> by burning fuel. Most rocket engines turn the fuel into hot gas. Pushing the gas out of the back of the engine makes the rocket move forward." [5]

Photo Credit: NASA

<u>Thrust</u> – "The forward or upward force produced by the engines of a plane or rocket." [6]

Are there different types of rocket engines?

Yes, "there are two main types of rocket engines. Some rockets use liquid fuel." [7] "Other rockets use solid fuels." [8] "Fireworks and model rockets also fly using solid fuels." [9]

"On the side of the Space Shuttle are two white solid rocket boosters. They use solid fuels." [10] "The solid rocket boosters looked like two thin rockets. They gave the rocket the lift from Earth's gravity." [11]

The Space Shuttle also had an external, orange 'liquid fuel' tank. This external tank provided liquid fuel to the Space Shuttle 'Main Engines'.

Liquid Fuel Tank

Solid Rocket Engine

Solid Rocket Engine

Space Shuttle 'Main Engines' operated with liquid fuel.

Photo Credit: NASA

When were rockets invented?

"The mighty space rockets of today are the result of [many] years of invention, experimentation, and discovery."[12]

"The first known rockets were used in China in the 1200s [over 800 years ago]. These solid rockets were used for fireworks." [13]

Photo Credit: Pixabay

What was the Saturn V?

"The Saturn V was a NASA rocket. (The V in the name is the Roman numeral five.) This rocket launched astronauts to the moon. The Saturn V was used in the Apollo program in the 1960s and 1970s. It also launched the Skylab space station." [14] The Skylab space station had a workspace and space observatory for astronauts as well as other equipment for scientific research.

Saturn V Launch of Skylab 3

Photo Credit: NASA

Skylab Space Station

Photo Credit: NASA

How big was the Saturn V?

Photo Credit: Pixabay

Photo Credit: NASA

"The Saturn V rocket was about as tall as a 36-story-tall building. It was taller than the Statue of Liberty. Full of fuel, the Saturn V weighed about the same as 400 elephants." [15]

Did Saturn V Launches always carry astronauts?

No. In order to ensure the safety of astronauts participating in the Saturn V Program, "the first Saturn Vs launched without crews. These were just test launches to make sure the Saturn V rocket worked like scientists wanted" [16] before astronauts were actually carried by the Saturn V launch vehicle into space.

Photo Credit: NASA

What was the Apollo Program?

Managed by the National Aeronautics Space Administration (NASA), the mission of the Apollo Program was to send astronauts to the moon. "There were 11 Apollo flights. The first Apollo flight was in 1968." [17] Out of the 11 Apollo space flights that were made, the "first four flights tested the spacecraft. Six of the other seven flights landed on the moon. The first moon landing took place in 1969. The last moon landing was in 1972." [18]

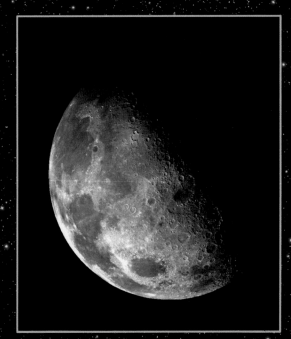

Photo Credit: NASA

What was the 'Lunar Module'?

The Lunar Module was a spacecraft used for landing on the moon. It "carried two astronauts... [and] took them from orbit around the moon to the moon's surface." [19] "Twelve astronauts walked on the moon. They studied the lunar surface. They collected moon rocks and brought them back to Earth." [20]

Photo Credit: NASA

What was the Space Shuttle?

Photo Credit: NASA

"The Space Shuttle was NASA's space transportation system. It carried astronauts and cargo... from Earth [to outer space]. The first space shuttle flight took place April 12, 1981. The shuttle made its final landing July 21, 2011. During those 30 years, the Space Shuttle launched on 135 missions." [21]

How many astronauts could the Space Shuttle carry?

Photo Credit: NASA

Photo Credit: NASA

The Space Shuttle "could carry up to seven astronauts at a time." [22]

Did the Space Shuttle carry spacecraft and supplies into space?

Yes, the "Space Shuttle was like a moving van. It took satellites to space so they could orbit Earth." [23] The Space Shuttle also "carried large parts into space to build the International Space Station." [24] On July 4, 2006, the "Space Shuttle Discovery and its seven-member crew traveled to the International Space Station... [to deliver] supplies and make repairs to the space station." [25]

Space Shuttle Discovery (STS-121) Launches on Supply Mission to International Space Station

Photo Credit: NASA

International Space Station

Photo Credit: NASA

What did the Space Shuttle do?

Photo Credit: NASA

The Space Shuttle was designed to do many things. "The Space Shuttle was... like a science lab. Astronauts did experiments there. Doing experiments in space is different than doing them on Earth." [26] In addition, Space Shuttle astronauts did repair and maintenance on spacecraft, as well.

What were the large parts of the Space Shuttle design?

"The Space Shuttle was made of three main parts: the orbiter, the external tank, and the solid rocket boosters. The orbiter was the part that looked like an airplane. The orbiter flew around Earth. The astronauts rode and lived in this part. NASA had five orbiters. The names of the orbiters [that flew into space] were Atlantis, Challenger, Columbia, Discovery, and Endeavour." [27]

External Fuel Tank

Solid Rocket Booster

Shuttle Orbiter

Photo Credit: NASA

How did the Space Shuttle launch and land?

"The Space Shuttle launched like a rocket. When it returned to Earth, it came down from the sky and landed like a glider airplane." [28]

Space Shuttle Atlantis (STS-66) Landing at Edwards Air Force Base, California

Photo Credit: NASA

Space Shuttle Atlantis (STS-135) Launching from Kennedy Space Center, Florida

Photo Credit: NASA

Pictorial History of Rockets

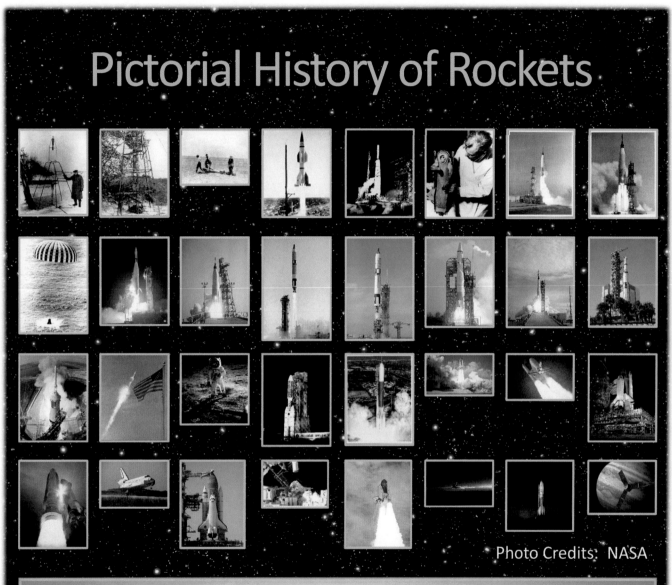

Photo Credits: NASA

The following 28 pages of this book provide a sampling of various research, development, and acquisition programs surrounding the history of rockets. The pictures with the accompanying facts form a rocket history timeline that depicts significant advances in rocket science as well as other interesting developments.

First Flight of a Liquid Propellant Rocket

(March 16, 1926) This is a photograph of "Dr. Robert H. Goddard and a liquid oxygen-gasoline rocket in the frame from which it was fired on March 16, 1926, at Auburn, Massachusetts. From 1930 to 1941, Dr. Goddard made substantial progress in the development of progressively larger rockets. In many respects, Dr. Goddard laid the essential foundations of practical rocket technology." [29]

Photo Credit: NASA

Fourth Flight of a Liquid Propellant Rocket

(July 17, 1929) "Dr. Robert H. Goddard's rocket is in the tower, ready for... test at Auburn, Massachusetts. This was the fourth flight of a liquid-propellant rocket. Rocks were piled on pipes directly under the nozzle, on a frame suspended from the two 3/8 inch pipe guides to keep the... [structure] as straight as possible by the tension produced in this way. The noise from this particular rocket launch attracted the attention of the entire community. When the public grew concerned over the potential hazards of the rockets, Goddard was forced to conduct his test flights on the Army artillery range at Camp Devens, Massachusetts." [30]

Photo Credit: NASA

Dr. Robert H. Goddard's Rocket After Flight

Photo Credit: NASA

(April 19, 1932) This is a photograph of "Dr. Robert H. Goddard's rocket after flight in New Mexico." [31] "In 1930, with a grant from the Guggenheim Foundation, Goddard and his crew moved from Massachusetts to Roswell, New Mexico, to conduct research and perform test flights away from the public eye. This rocket was one of many that he launched in Roswell from 1930-1932 and from 1934-1941. Dr. Goddard has been recognized as the father of American rocketry and as one of the pioneers in the theoretical exploration of space. His dream was the conquest of the upper atmosphere and ultimately space through the use of rocket propulsion." [32]

Hermes A-1 Test Rocket

(May 1, 1950) "The first Hermes A-1 test rocket was fired at White Sand Proving Ground (WSPG). Hermes was a modified V-2 German rocket, utilizing the German aerodynamic configuration; however, internally it was a completely new design. Although it did not result in an operational vehicle, the information that was gathered in the process contributed directly to the development of the Redstone rocket." [33] "The first Redstone rocket was launched at Cape Canaveral, Florida, on August 20, 1953." [34]

Hermes A-1 Rocket

First Redstone Rocket Firing

Photo Credits: NASA

Pioneer I on the Launch Pad

(October 11, 1958). This is a picture of the "Thor-Able I with the Pioneer I spacecraft atop, prior to launch at Eastern Test Range at what is now Kennedy Space Center. Pioneer I... [was] the first spacecraft launched by the 11 day old National Aeronautics and Space Administration [NASA]. Although it failed to reach the Moon, it did transmit 43 hours of data." [35]

Photo Credit: NASA

Sam the Monkey After His Ride in the Little Joe 2 Spacecraft

(December 4, 1959) This is a photograph of "Sam, the Rhesus monkey, after his ride in the Little Joe-2 (LJ-2) spacecraft. A U.S. Navy destroyer safely recovered Sam after he experienced three minutes of weightlessness during the flight. Animals were often used during test flights for Project Mercury to help determine the effects of spaceflight and weightlessness on humans. LJ-2 was one in a series of flights that led up to the human orbital flights of NASA's Project Mercury program." [36]

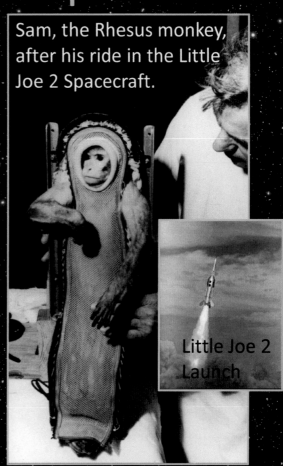

Sam, the Rhesus monkey, after his ride in the Little Joe 2 Spacecraft.

Little Joe 2 Launch

Photo Credits: NASA

Launch of Mercury-Atlas

(February 21, 1961) In this Project Mercury test, a spacecraft boosted by a modified Atlas was launched from Cape Canaveral, Florida. The Mercury capsule reached a peak altitude of 107... miles and landed 1.425 miles down range." [37]

"Project SCORE, the first communications satellite that transmitted President Eisenhower's pre-recorded Christmas speech around the world, was launched on an Atlas." [38]

Photo Credit: NASA

SCORE – SCORE stands for "Signal Communications by Orbiting Relay Equipment".

Mercury-Atlas 3 Test Launch

(April 25, 1961) "A NASA Project Mercury spacecraft was test launched at 11:15 AM EST on April 25, 1961 from Cape Canaveral, Florida, in a test designed to qualify the Mercury Spacecraft and all systems, which must function during orbit and reentry from orbit. The Mercury-Atlas vehicle was destroyed by [a] Range Safety Officer about 40 seconds after liftoff. The spacecraft was recovered and appeared to be in good condition." [39]

Photo Credit: NASA

Little Joe 5B Test Launch

(April 28, 1961) After being launched by a Little Joe 5B rocket booster, a Mercury spacecraft with its "ring-sail parachute lands... off the shore of Wallops Island, Virginia. The Little Joe rocket booster was developed as a cheaper, smaller, and more functional alternative to the Redstone rockets. Little Joe could be produced at one-fifth the cost of Redstone rockets and still have enough power to carry a capsule payload. Seven unmanned Little Joe rockets were launched at Wallops Island, Virginia, from August 1959 to April 1961." [40]

Mercury Spacecraft Landing

Little Joe 5B Launch

Photo Credits: NASA

Mariner 1 Launch

(July 22, 1962) This is a picture of an "Atlas-Agena 5 carrying the Mariner 1 spacecraft lifting off from Cape Kennedy Launch Complex 12. The Mariner spacecraft was scheduled to orbit Venus." [41]

Photo Credit: NASA

Mercury-Atlas 9 Launches Faith 7

(May 15, 1963) "Mercury-Atlas 9 lifts off from Pad 14 at Cape Canaveral with astronaut L. Gordon Cooper aboard Faith 7 for what was then the nation's longest manned orbital flight. Lift-off occurred at 8:04 a.m. EST, on May 15, 1963. And 34 hours, 20 minutes, 30 seconds, and 22 orbits later, Gordon Cooper was resting in his Faith 7 space capsule in the... Pacific Ocean." [42]

Photo Credit: NASA

Gemini-Titan 4 (GT-4) Launch

(June 3, 1965) This is a picture of the "Gemini-Titan 4 (GT-4) lift-off from... [Launch Complex 19 at Cape Canaveral Air Force Station, Florida]. This flight included the first spacewalk by an American astronaut." [43]

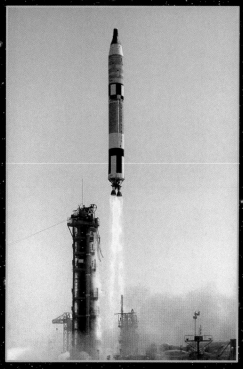

Photo Credit: NASA

Gemini VI Launch

(December 15, 1965) "The Gemini VI, scheduled as a two-day mission, was launched... [from Launch Complex 19 at Cape Canaveral Air Force Station, Florida]. Gemini VI rendezvoused with Gemini VII, already orbiting the Earth." [44]

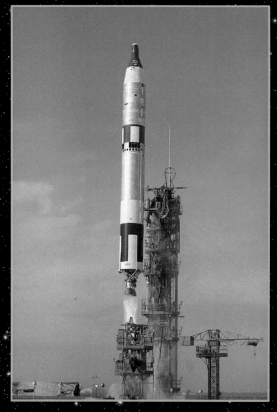

Photo Credit: NASA

Surveyor 1 Launch

(May 30, 1966) This is a photograph of "The Atlas-Centaur 10, carrying the Surveyor 1 spacecraft, lifting off from [Launch Complex 36A at Cape Canaveral Air Force Station, Florida]. Surveyor 1, the first of a series of seven robotic spacecraft sent to the moon to gather data in preparation for NASA's Apollo missions, was the first spacecraft to make a true soft landing on the moon. As such, it was one of the great successes of NASA's early lunar and interplanetary program." [45]

"Over a period of about 30 days, Surveyor 1 transmitted more than 11,000 photographs as well as data on the moon's surface and temperature." [46]

Surveyor 1 Launch

Photo Credit: NASA

(November 20, 1969) "Charles Conrad Jr., Apollo 12 Commander, examines the unmanned Surveyor III spacecraft during the second extravehicular activity (EVA-2). The Lunar Module (LM) "Intrepid" is in the right background. This picture was taken by astronaut Alan L. Bean, Lunar Module pilot. The 'Intrepid' landed on the Moon's Ocean of Storms only 600 feet from Surveyor III. The television camera and several other components were taken from Surveyor III and brought back to earth for scientific analysis. Surveyor III soft-landed on the Moon on April 19, 1967." [47]

Surveyor III Examined on Moon by Apollo 12 Astronaut

Photo Credit: NASA

Atlas-Agena Target Vehicle Launch

(September 12, 1966) The photograph on the right is the "Atlas-Agena target vehicle liftoff for Gemini 11 from [Launch Complex] 14 at Cape Canaveral Air Force Station, Florida. Once the Agena was in orbit, Gemini 11 rendezvoused and docked with it." [48]

Atlas-Agena Target Vehicle Liftoff

Photo Credit: NASA

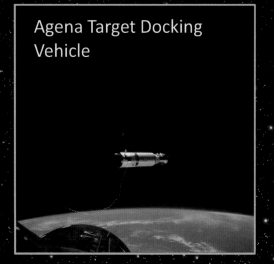

Agena Target Docking Vehicle

Photo Credit: NASA

(September 12, 1966) "The Agena Target Docking Vehicle at a distance of approximately 80 feet from the Gemini-11 spacecraft. This view was taken after the disconnect of the tether between the two vehicles." [49]

Apollo 10 Mission

(March 11, 1969) This is a picture of the "Apollo 10 rollout from the Vehicle Assembly Building (VAB) to Launch Complex 39B. This mission launched on May 18, 1969." [50]

"Apollo 10 was the fourth manned mission in the United States Apollo space program. [The purpose of the Apollo 10 mission] was to be a dress rehearsal for the Apollo 11 mission, testing all of the procedures and components of a Moon landing without actually landing on the Moon itself." [51]

Apollo 10 Rollout

Apollo 10 Helicopter Recovery Operation

Apollo 10 Launch

Photo Credits: NASA

Apollo 11 Mission

(July 16, 1969) "At 9:32 a.m. EDT, the swing arms move away and a plume of flame signals the liftoff of the Apollo 11 Saturn V space vehicle and astronauts Neil A. Armstrong, Michael Collins, and Edwin E. Aldrin, Jr. from Kennedy Space Center Launch Complex 39A." [52] "Apollo 11 was the Apollo program mission that landed the first humans on the Moon... [and in doing so] fulfilled a national goal proposed in 1961 by the late US President John F. Kennedy in a speech before the United States Congress, 'before this decade is out, of landing a man on the Moon and returning him safely to the Earth.' " [53]

Photo Credit: NASA

Apollo 11 Launch

(July 16, 1969) "The American flag heralds the flight of Apollo 11, the first Lunar landing mission." [54]

"During the planned eight-day mission, [Neil A.] Armstrong and [Edwin E.] Aldrin will descend in a Lunar Module to the Moon's surface while [Michael] Collins orbits overhead in the Command Module. The two astronauts are to spend 22 hours on the Moon, including two and one-half hours outside the lunar module. They will gather samples of lunar material and will deploy scientific experiments which will transmit data about the lunar environment. They will rejoin Collins in the Command Module for the return trip to Earth." [55]

Photo Credit: NASA

Apollo 11 Lands a Man on the Moon

Astronaut Buzz Aldrin, lunar module pilot, walks on the surface of the Moon.

(July 20, 1969) "On July 20, 1969, Astronauts Neil Armstrong and Buzz Aldrin became the first humans to step onto the lunar surface. Together they collected 47.5 pounds of lunar material for return to Earth. Michael Collins piloted the command spacecraft alone in lunar orbit until Armstrong and Aldrin returned to it just under a day later for the trip back to Earth." [56]

Photo Credit: NASA

Voyager 2 Launch

(August 20, 1977) Voyager 2 is a spacecraft "designed to study the outer <u>solar system</u> and then <u>interstellar</u> space." [57] "The initial mission plan for Voyager 2 specified visits only to Jupiter and Saturn. The plan was augmented [4 years later] in 1981 to include a visit to Uranus, and again in 1985 to include a flyby of Neptune. After completing the tour of the outer planets in 1989, the Voyager spacecraft began exploring <u>interstellar</u> space. The Voyager mission has been managed by NASA's Office of Space Science and the Jet Propulsion Laboratory" [58] and is "expected to continue transmitting radio messages until 2025." [59]

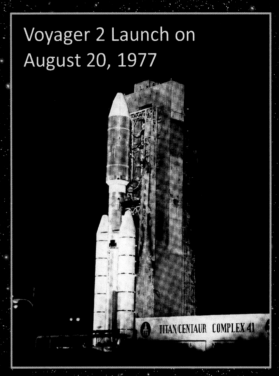

Voyager 2 Launch on August 20, 1977

Photo Credit: NASA [61]

Artist Concept of Voyager 2

Photo Credit: NASA [60]

1. <u>Solar System</u> - "The sun together with all the planets and other bodies that revolve around it." (Dictionary.com) [62]
2. <u>Interstellar</u> - "Situated or occurring between the stars." (Dictionary.com) [63]

Delta 174 Launch

Delta 174 Launch from Cape Canaveral Air Force Station, Florida, on March 1, 1984.

(March 1, 1984) "The Delta launch vehicle family started development in 1959. The Delta was composed of parts from the Thor, an intermediate-range ballistic missile, as its first stage, and the Vanguard as its second. The first Delta was launched from Cape Canaveral on May 13, 1960." [64] "Delta has been used to launch civil, commercial, and military satellites into orbit." [65]

Photo Credit: NASA

Space Shuttle Challenger (<u>STS</u> 61-A)

(October 30, 1985) "The Space Shuttle Challenger blasted off at noon EDT from the launch pad at Complex 39, Kennedy Space Center." [66] "Within hours of this photo, the Spacelab D-1 Science Module was activated and crew members were busy performing experiments." [67]

<u>STS</u>: The acronym 'STS' stands for the Space Shuttle 'Space Transportation System' (STS).

Space Shuttle Atlantis (STS-27)

Photo Credit: NASA

(December 2, 1988) "Space Shuttle Atlantis takes flight on its STS-27 mission... utilizing 375,000 pounds [of] thrust produced by its three main engines. The STS-27 was the third classified mission dedicated to the Department of Defense (DoD). After completion of [the] mission, Orbiter Atlantis landed December 6, 1988, 3:36 p.m. PST at Edwards Air Force Base, California." [68]

Space Shuttle Columbia (STS-28)

(July 15, 1989) "The Space Shuttle Columbia arrives at Pad 39B early in the morning after being rolled out of the Vehicle Assembly Building the night before. Columbia is scheduled for Launch on Space Shuttle Mission STS-28 in late July on a Department of Defense dedicated mission." [69]

Photo Credit: NASA

An Interesting Note of Trivia: The Space Shuttle Columbia was the first Space Shuttle to orbit and return to Earth. It launched on April 12, 1981. After orbiting the Earth a total of 36 times, it returned back to Earth on April 14, 1981.

Space Shuttle Discovery (STS-70)

(July 13 and July 22, 1995) After launching July 13, 1995, Space Shuttle Discovery (STS-70) "landed at the Kennedy Space Center on July 22, 1995]." [70] "STS-70 was the first shuttle mission controlled from the new mission control center room at Johnson Space Center [in Houston, Texas]." [71]

Space Shuttle Discovery (STS-70) Launch (July 13, 1995)

Photo Credit: NASA

Space Shuttle Discovery (STS-70) Landing (July 22, 1995)

Photo Credit: NASA

Space Shuttle Endeavour (STS-127)

(July 11, 2009) In the photograph to the right, "The Space Shuttle Endeavour is seen at launch pad 39A at NASA's Kennedy Space Center in Cape Canaveral, Florida" [72] as it prepares for launch on July 15, 2009.

(July 22, 2009) In the photograph below, "Astronaut Christopher Cassidy, STS-127 mission specialist, is pictured during Endeavour's third space walk of a scheduled five overall for this flight." [73]

Photo Credit: NASA

Photo Credit: NASA

Final Space Shuttle Mission STS-135 Atlantis Launch and Landing

(July 8, 2011) "Space Shuttle Atlantis' STS-135 mission launched from Launch Pad 39A at Kennedy Space Center. STS-135 was the last Space Shuttle mission."[74]

(July 21, 2011) "Space Shuttle Atlantis (STS-135) touches down at NASA's Kennedy Space Center Shuttle Landing Facility (SLF), completing its 13-day mission to the International Space Station (ISS) and the final flight of the Space Shuttle Program, early Thursday morning, July 21, 2011, in Cape Canaveral, Florida. Overall, Atlantis spent 307 days in space and traveled nearly 126 million miles during its 33 flights. Atlantis, the fourth orbiter built, launched on its first mission on Oct. 3, 1985."[75]

Space Shuttle Atlantis (STS-135) Launch (July 8, 2011)

Photo Credit: NASA

Space Shuttle Atlantis (STS-135) Landing (July 21, 2011)

Photo Credit: NASA/Bill Ingalls

Atlas V Rocket Ready for Juno Mission

Atlas V Rocket with Juno Spacecraft is Ready for Launch

Juno Spacecraft Orbiting Planet Jupiter

Photo Credit: NASA [77]

Photo Credit: NASA/JPL-Caltech [78]

(August 4, 2011) "An Atlas V rocket with NASA's Juno spacecraft payload is seen the evening before it's planned launch at Space Launch Complex 41 of the Cape Canaveral Air Force Station in Florida on Thursday, August 4, 2011. The Juno spacecraft [was launched on] a five-year, 400-million-mile voyage to Jupiter, orbit the planet... [and use] eight instruments to probe its internal structure and gravity field, measure water and ammonia in its atmosphere, map its powerful magnetic field, and observe its intense auroras". [76]

Auroras – Auroras appear like glowing lights in the planet's atmosphere.

-- PHOTO QUIZ GAME --
What Apollo mission landed the first humans on the Moon?

Apollo 4

Photo Credit: NASA

Apollo 11

Photo Credit: NASA

Apollo 12

Photo Credit: NASA

Apollo 14

Photo Credit: NASA

ANSWER: As part of the Apollo 11 mission, Astronauts Neil Armstrong and Buzz Aldrin became the first humans to step onto the surface of the Moon on July 20, 1969.

What was the name of the rocket booster that launched Sam (the Rhesus monkey) during test flights for Project Mercury to help determine the effects of spaceflight and weightlessness on humans?

Photo Credit: NASA

Hermes

Photo Credit: NASA

Little Joe

Photo Credit: NASA

Thor-Able

Photo Credit: NASA

Atlas

Photo Credit: NASA

ANSWER: The 'Little Joe' rocket booster was used to launch Sam (the Rhesus monkey) in a series of test flights for Project Mercury to help determine the effects of spaceflight and weightlessness on humans. The 'Little Joe' test flights eventually led up to the human orbital flights of NASA's Project Mercury program.

What is the name of the orbiter that completed the final flight of the 30-Year Space Shuttle Program?

Endeavour

Photo Credit: NASA

Columbia

Photo Credit: NASA

Challenger

Photo Credit: NASA

Discovery

Photo Credit: NASA

Atlantis

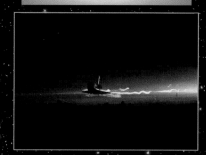

Photo Credit: NASA/Bill Ingalls

ANSWER: The Space Shuttle orbiter Atlantis completed the final flight of the 30-year Space Shuttle Program on July 21, 2011 when it landed at Cape Canaveral, Florida.

Rocket Launches Crossword Puzzle

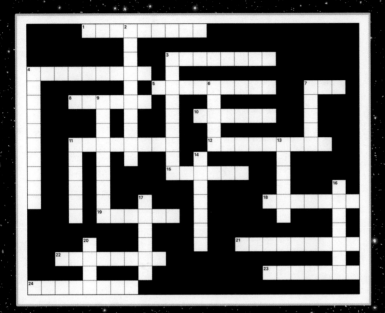

Answers to the Rocket Launches Crossword Puzzle can be found throughout the various pages of this book. In case you cannot locate the answers, they are also shown on the back side of this page, as well.

Across

1. Space Shuttle orbiter; finding, detection, sighting
3. First Space Shuttle to orbit and return to earth
4. Astronaut's mission in outer space
5. Retired orbiter of the Space Shuttle Program
7. Name of the Rhesus Monkey that flew test flights in support of the Mercury Space Program
8. Mars or Venus
10. Pre-Apollo program
11. Robotic spacecraft that was used to demonstrate feasibility of soft landings on the Moon
12. Last name of Moonwalker Neil
15. Cape Canaveral event
18. First mission to put an American astronaut in space
19. Rocket propulsion
21. Earth orbiter
22. Lunar stroll
23. Last name of the father of modern rocketry
24. Name of the Space Shuttle orbiter that flew the final mission of the Space Shuttle Program

Down

2. Famed Space Shuttle
3. Florida cape where rocket launches occur
4. Mariner 4 or Voyager 2
6. Gemini docking target space vehicle
7. Number of astronauts that could be carried by a Space Shuttle orbiter
9. Spacesuit donner
11. Apollo-era NASA rocket
13. Blast off. Atlas, Titan, Redstone, etc.
14. Largest planet
16. Space Shuttle component
17. Space telescope name
20. Apollo 11's destination

Rocket Launches Crossword Puzzle (with Answers)

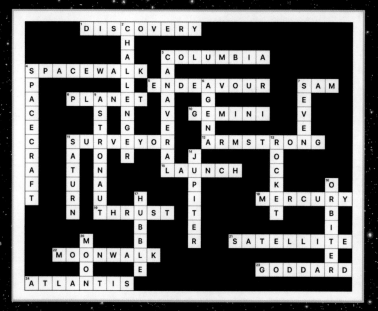

Answers to the Rocket Launches Crossword Puzzle located on the previous page are revealed here as well as throughout the various pages of this book.

Across
1. Space Shuttle orbiter; finding, detection, sighting
3. First Space Shuttle to orbit and return to earth
4. Astronaut's mission in outer space
5. Retired orbiter of the Space Shuttle Program
7. Name of the Rhesus Monkey that flew test flights in support of the Mercury Space Program
8. Mars or Venus
10. Pre-Apollo program
11. Robotic spacecraft that was used to demonstrate feasibility of soft landings on the Moon
12. Last name of Moonwalker Neil
15. Cape Canaveral event
18. First mission to put an American astronaut in space
19. Rocket propulsion
21. Earth orbiter
22. Lunar stroll
23. Last name of the father of modern rocketry
24. Name of the Space Shuttle orbiter that flew the final mission of the Space Shuttle Program

Down
2. Famed Space Shuttle
3. Florida cape where rocket launches occur
4. Mariner 4 or Voyager 2
6. Gemini docking target space vehicle
7. Number of astronauts that could be carried by a Space Shuttle orbiter
9. Spacesuit donner
11. Apollo-era NASA rocket
13. Blast off. Atlas, Titan, Redstone, etc.
14. Largest planet
16. Space Shuttle component
17. Space telescope name
20. Apollo 11's destination

Space Shuttle Coloring Page

Photo Credit: NASA

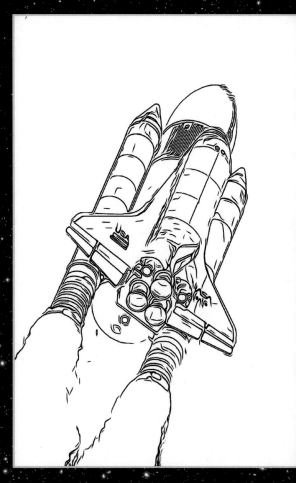

Colored by: _____

Date: _____

Juno Spacecraft Coloring Page

Photo Credit:
NASA/JPL-Caltech

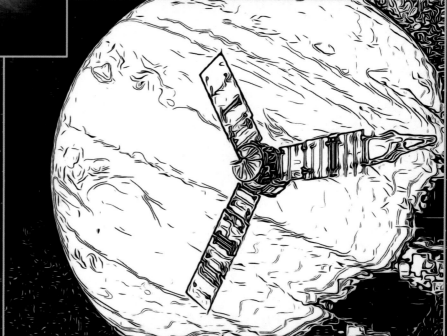

Colored by: _____

Date: _____

-- EXTRA BONUS SECTION --
"MOONWALKS"

Photographic Image of the Moon

Apollo 11 Bootprint on the Surface of the Moon

Photo Credit: NASA [80]

Photo Credit: NASA [81]

Walking on the moon is commonly referred to as a 'moonwalk'. "A total of 12 astronauts have walked on the Moon's surface, all during the Apollo Program of the late 1960s and early 1970s." [79]

Eagle Lunar Module In Lunar Orbit over the Moon

(July 20, 1969) "The Apollo 11 Lunar Module (LM) Eagle', in a landing configuration is photographed in lunar orbit from the Command and Service Modules (CSM) 'Columbia'. Inside the LM were Commander Neil A. Armstrong and Lunar Module Pilot Edwin E. 'Buzz' Aldrin, Jr. The long 'rod-like' protrusions under the landing pods are lunar surface sensing probes. Upon contact with the lunar surface, the probes send a signal to the crew to shut down the descent engine." [82]

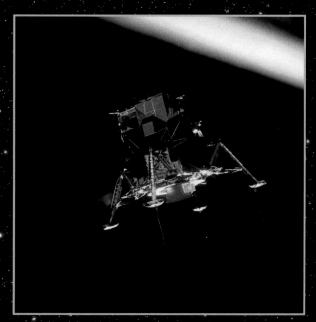

Photo Credit: NASA

Descending the Lunar Module to the Moon's Surface

(November 19, 1969). "Alan L. Bean, Lunar Module pilot for the Apollo 12 mission, starts down the ladder of the Lunar Module (LM) "Intrepid" to join astronaut Charles Conrad, Jr., mission Commander, on the lunar surface." [83]

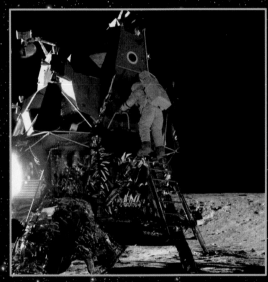

Photo Credit: NASA

Saluting the U.S. Flag on the Moon

(April 21, 1972) "Astronaut John W. Young, commander of the Apollo 16 lunar landing mission, jumps up from the lunar surface as he salutes the U.S. Flag at the Descartes landing site during the first Apollo 16 extravehicular activity (EVA-1). Astronaut Charles M. Duke, Jr., lunar module pilot, took this picture. The Lunar Module (LM) 'Orion' is on the left. The Lunar Roving Vehicle is parked beside the LM. The object behind Young in the shade of the LM is the Far Ultraviolet Camera / Spectrograph. Stone Mountain dominates the background in this lunar scene." [84]

Photo Credit: NASA

Driving the Lunar Roving Vehicle on the Moon

(December 11, 1972) "Astronaut Eugene A. Cernan, Apollo 17 mission commander, makes a short checkout of the Lunar Roving Vehicle during the early part of the first Apollo 17 extravehicular activity (EVA-1) at the Taurus-Littrow landing site." [85]

Photo Credit: NASA

Exploring the Moon's Surface

(December 13, 1972) "Geologist-Astronaut Harrison H. Schmitt is photographed standing next to a huge, split boulder at Station 6 on the sloping base of North Massif during the third Apollo 17 extravehicular activity (EVA-3) at the Taurus-Littrow landing site. The 'Rover' Lunar Roving Vehicle (LRV) is in the left foreground. Schmitt is the Apollo 17 Lunar Module pilot. This picture was taken by Commander Eugene A. Cernan." [86]

Photo Credit: NASA

Collecting Soil from the Surface of the Moon

(August 2, 1971) "Astronaut James B. Irwin, lunar module pilot, uses a scoop in making a trench in the lunar soil during Apollo 15 extravehicular activity (EVA)." [87]

"During moonwalks, experiments were often set up and rocks and other materials from the Moon's surface collected." [88]

Photo Credit: NASA

Footnote References

1. Dictionary.com website. "Definition of Rocket". Retrieved on July 28, 2018, from https://www.dictionary.com/browse/rocket?s=t
2. "Rockets Educator Guide". Rockets Introductory Pages. Retrieved on July 28, 2018, from https://www.nasa.gov/pdf/153411main_Rockets_Intro_Pages.pdf
3. Dictionary.com website. "Definition of Satellite". Retrieved on July 28, 2018, from https://www.dictionary.com/browse/satellite?s=ts
4. Dictionary.com website. "Definition of Spacecraft". Retrieved on July 28, 2018, from https://www.dictionary.com/browse/spacecraft?s=t
5. "What is a Rocket?" NASA Knows! (Grades 5-8) article series (September 21, 2010). Retrieved on July 8, 2018, from https://www.nasa.gov/audience/forstudents/5-8/features/nasa-knows/what-is-a-rocket-58.html
6. Ibid.
7. Ibid.
8. Ibid.
9. Ibid.
10. Ibid.
11. "What was the Space Shuttle?" NASA Knows! (Grades 5-8) article series (November 26, 2013). Retrieved on July 8, 2018, from https://www.nasa.gov/audience/forstudents/5-8/features/nasa-knows/what-is-the-space-shuttle-58.html
12. "Pictorial History of Rockets". Retrieved on July 28, 2018, from https://www.nasa.gov/pdf/153410main_Rockets_History.pdf
13. Ibid.
14. "What was the Saturn V?" NASA Knows! (Grades K-4) article series (September 17, 2010). Retrieved on July 8, 2018, from https://www.nasa.gov/audience/forstudents/k-4/stories/nasa-knows/what-was-the-saturn-v-k4.html
15. Ibid.
16. Ibid.
17. "What was the Apollo Program?" NASA Knows! (Grades K-4) article series (July 19, 2017). Retrieved on July 8, 2018, from https://www.nasa.gov/audience/forstudents/k-4/stories/nasa-knows/what-was-apollo-program-k4.html
18. Ibid.
19. Ibid.
20. Ibid.
21. "What was the Space Shuttle?" NASA Knows! (Grades 5-8) article series (November 26, 2013). Retrieved on July 8, 2018, from https://www.nasa.gov/audience/forstudents/5-8/features/nasa-knows/what-is-the-space-shuttle-58.html
22. Ibid.
23. "What was the Space Shuttle?" NASA Knows! (Grades K-4) article series (November 26, 2013). Retrieved on July 8, 2018, https://www.nasa.gov/audience/forstudents/k-4/stories/nasa-knows/what-is-the-space-shuttle-k4.html
24. Ibid.
25. NASA on the Commons Photo Album "International Space Station". Retrieved on July 14, 2018, from https://www.flickr.com/photos/nasacommons/albums/72157648186433655/with/ 15357921727/
26. "What was the Space Shuttle?" NASA Knows! (Grades K-4) article series (November 26, 2013). Retrieved on July 14, 2018, from https://www.nasa.gov/audience/forstudents/k-4/stories/nasa-knows/what-is-the-space-shuttle-k4.html
27. Ibid.
28. Ibid.
29. NASA on the Commons Photo Album "Rocket Launches". Retrieved on July 8, 2018, from https://www.flickr.com/photos/nasacommons/albums/72157650354621478
30. Ibid.
31. Ibid.
32. Ibid.
33. Ibid.
34. Ibid.
35. Ibid.
36. Ibid.
37. Ibid.
38. Ibid.
39. NASA on the Commons Photo Album "Rocket Launches". Retrieved on July 8, 2018, from https://www.flickr.com/photos/nasacommons/albums/72157650354621478
40. Ibid.
41. Ibid.
42. Ibid.

Footnote References (continued)

43. NASA on the Commons Photo Album "Rocket Launches". Retrieved on July 8, 2018, from https://www.flickr.com/photos/nasacommons/albums/72157650354621478
44. Ibid.
45. Ibid.
46. Ibid.
47. NASA on the Commons Photo Album "Apollo 12". Retrieved on July 15, 2018, from
    https://www.flickr.com/photos/nasacommons/albums/72157634967531957/with/30658166262/
48. NASA on the Commons Photo Album "Rocket Launches". Retrieved on July 8, 2018, from https://www.flickr.com/photos/nasacommons/albums/72157650354621478
49. NASA on the Commons Photo Album "Apollo 12". Retrieved on July 15, 2018, from
    https://www.flickr.com/photos/nasacommons/albums/72157634967531957/with/30658166262/
50. NASA on the Commons Photo Album "Apollo 10". Retrieved on July 15, 2018, from
    https://www.flickr.com/photos/nasacommons/albums/72157634967503435/with/9460177260/
51. Ibid.
52. NASA on the Commons Photo Album "Apollo 11". Retrieved on July 15, 2018, from
    https://www.flickr.com/photos/nasacommons/albums/72157634973926806/with/7610985944/
53. Ibid.
54. Ibid.
55. Ibid.
56. Ibid.
57. NASA on the Commons Photo Album "NASA ArtSpace". Retrieved on July 15, 2018, from https://www.flickr.com/photos/nasacommons/albums/72157633936061500
58. NASA on the Commons Photo Album "Voyager and Galileo". Retrieved on July 26, 2018, from
    https://www.flickr.com/photos/nasacommons/albums/72157634969190665/with/9460966900/
59. NASA on the Commons Photo Album "NASA ArtSpace". Retrieved on July 15, 2018, from https://www.flickr.com/photos/nasacommons/albums/72157633936061500
60. Ibid.
61. NASA on the Commons Photo Album "Voyager and Galileo". Retrieved on July 26, 2018, from https://www.flickr.com/photos/nasacommons/albums/72157634969190665/
    with/9460966900/
62. Dictionary.com website. "Definition of Solar System". Retrieved on July 28, 2018, from https://www.dictionary.com/browse/solar-system?s=t
63. Dictionary.com website. "Definition of Interstellar". Retrieved on July 28, 2018, from https://www.dictionary.com/browse/interstellar?s=t
64. NASA on the Commons Photo Album "Rocket Launches". Retrieved on July 8, 2018, from https://www.flickr.com/photos/nasacommons/albums/72157650354621478
65. Ibid.
66. Ibid.
67. Ibid.
68. Ibid.
69. NASA on the Commons Photo Album "Space Shuttle Columbia". Retrieved on July 15, 2018, from
    https://www.flickr.com/photos/nasacommons/albums/72157650279651165
70. NASA on the Commons Photo Album "Space Shuttle Discovery". Retrieved on July 15, 2018, from
    https://www.flickr.com/photos/nasacommons/albums/72157634969316957
71. Ibid.
72. NASA on the Commons Photo Album "Space Shuttle Endeavor". Retrieved on 15 July 2018 from
    https://www.flickr.com/photos/nasacommons/albums/72157634975802990/
73. Ibid.
74. NASA on the Commons Photo Album "Space Shuttle Atlantis". Retrieved on 14 July 2018 from
    https://www.flickr.com/photos/nasacommons/albums/72157634975731504/with/ 19143875390/
75. Ibid.
76. NASA on the Commons Photo Album "Rocket Launches". Retrieved on 8 July 2018 from https://www.flickr.com/photos/nasacommons/albums/72157650354621478
77. Ibid.
78. NASA on the Commons Photo Album "NASA ArtSpace". Retrieved on 15 July 2018 from https://www.flickr.com/photos/nasacommons/albums/72157633936061500
79. NASA on the Commons Photo Album "Moonwalks". Retrieved on 8 July 2018 from https://www.flickr.com/photos/nasacommons/albums/72157634974031758
80. NASA on the Commons Photo Album "Earth's Moon". Retrieved on 15 July 2018 from
    https://www.flickr.com/photos/nasacommons/albums/72157650639118181/with/9458193857/
81. NASA on the Commons Photo Album "Moonwalks". Retrieved on 8 July 2018 from https://www.flickr.com/photos/nasacommons/albums/72157634974031758
82. NASA on the Commons Photo Album "Lunar Module". Retrieved on 28 July 2018 from
    https://www.flickr.com/photos/nasacommons/albums/72157650733490842/with/9460192044/
83. NASA on the Commons Photo Album "Moonwalks". Retrieved on 8 July 2018 from https://www.flickr.com/photos/nasacommons/albums/72157634974031758
84. Ibid.
85. Ibid.
86. Ibid.
87. Ibid.
88. Ibid.

Check out our other interesting, fun-filled volumes from the
"All About This & That" Picture Book Series for Children!

Available now on Amazon!

83880289R00038